COFFEE BEAN

ENCYCLOPEDIA

ISBN-13: 978-1515305484
ISBN-10: 1515305481

How to Use This Book

Keeping track of passwords in today's electronic age is not an easy task. Of course, having a book sitting around that says 'internet passwords' is not a good idea. Fool your friends, family and co-workers with *Coffee Bean Encyclopedia, the Internet Password Book*!

To use this book, just follow the prompts for each section. Fill out as much information as you can for each website. It's best to write the information down at the same time you register on a new website. Each page is labeled in alphabetical order, so you can quickly flip to the appropriate page and find your login credentials for a particular website.

There is also a section in the back with handy tips for internet safety and protecting your online accounts.

Site URL:_____

Username:_____

Password:_____

Security Question Answer 1:_____

Security Question Answer 2:_____
NOTES:

Site URL:_____

Username:_____

Password:_____

Security Question Answer 1:_____

Security Question Answer 2:_____
NOTES:

Site URL:_____

Username:_____

Password:_____

Security Question Answer 1:_____

Security Question Answer 2:_____
NOTES:

Site URL:_____

Username:_____

Password:_____

Security Question Answer 1:_____

Security Question Answer 2:_____
NOTES:

Site URL:_____

Username:_____

Password:_____

Security Question Answer 1:_____

Security Question Answer 2:_____
NOTES:

Site URL:_____

Username:_____

Password:_____

Security Question Answer 1:_____

Security Question Answer 2:_____
NOTES:

Site URL:_____

Username:_____

Password:_____

Security Question Answer 1:_____

Security Question Answer 2:_____
NOTES:

Site URL:_____

Username:_____

Password:_____

Security Question Answer 1:_____

Security Question Answer 2:_____
NOTES:

Site URL:_____

Username:_____

Password:_____

Security Question Answer 1:_____

Security Question Answer 2:_____
NOTES:

Site URL:_____

Username:_____

Password:_____

Security Question Answer 1:_____

Security Question Answer 2:_____
NOTES:

Site URL:_____

Username:_____

Password:_____

Security Question Answer 1:_____

Security Question Answer 2:_____
NOTES:

Site URL:_____

Username:_____

Password:_____

Security Question Answer 1:_____

Security Question Answer 2:_____
NOTES:

Site URL:_____

Username:_____

Password:_____

Security Question Answer 1:_____

Security Question Answer 2:_____
NOTES:

Site URL:_____

Username:_____

Password:_____

Security Question Answer 1:_____

Security Question Answer 2:_____
NOTES:

Site URL:_____

Username:_____

Password:_____

Security Question Answer 1:_____

Security Question Answer 2:_____
NOTES:

Site URL:_____

Username:_____

Password:_____

Security Question Answer 1:_____

Security Question Answer 2:_____
NOTES:

Site URL:_____

Username:_____

Password:_____

Security Question Answer 1:_____

Security Question Answer 2:_____
NOTES:

Site URL:_____

Username:_____

Password:_____

Security Question Answer 1:_____

Security Question Answer 2:_____
NOTES:

Site URL:_____

Username:_____

Password:_____

Security Question Answer 1:_____

Security Question Answer 2:_____
NOTES:

Site URL:_____

Username:_____

Password:_____

Security Question Answer 1:_____

Security Question Answer 2:_____
NOTES:

Site URL:_____

Username:_____

Password:_____

Security Question Answer 1:_____

Security Question Answer 2:_____
NOTES:

Site URL:_____

Username:_____

Password:_____

Security Question Answer 1:_____

Security Question Answer 2:_____
NOTES:

Site URL:_____

Username:_____

Password:_____

Security Question Answer 1:_____

Security Question Answer 2:_____
NOTES:

Site URL:_____

Username:_____

Password:_____

Security Question Answer 1:_____

Security Question Answer 2:_____
NOTES:

Site URL:_____

Username:_____

Password:_____

Security Question Answer 1:_____

Security Question Answer 2:_____
NOTES:

Site URL:_____

Username:_____

Password:_____

Security Question Answer 1:_____

Security Question Answer 2:_____
NOTES:

Site URL:_____

Username:_____

Password:_____

Security Question Answer 1:_____

Security Question Answer 2:_____
NOTES:

Site URL:_____

Username:_____

Password:_____

Security Question Answer 1:_____

Security Question Answer 2:_____
NOTES:

Site URL:_____

Username:_____

Password:_____

Security Question Answer 1:_____

Security Question Answer 2:_____
NOTES:

Site URL:_____

Username:_____

Password:_____

Security Question Answer 1:_____

Security Question Answer 2:_____
NOTES:

Site URL:_____

Username:_____

Password:_____

Security Question Answer 1:_____

Security Question Answer 2:_____
NOTES:

Site URL:_____

Username:_____

Password:_____

Security Question Answer 1:_____

Security Question Answer 2:_____
NOTES:

Site URL:_____

Username:_____

Password:_____

Security Question Answer 1:_____

Security Question Answer 2:_____
NOTES:

Site URL:_____

Username:_____

Password:_____

Security Question Answer 1:_____

Security Question Answer 2:_____
NOTES:

Site URL:_____

Username:_____

Password:_____

Security Question Answer 1:_____

Security Question Answer 2:_____
NOTES:

Site URL:_____

Username:_____

Password:_____

Security Question Answer 1:_____

Security Question Answer 2:_____
NOTES:

Site URL:_____

Username:_____

Password:_____

Security Question Answer 1:_____

Security Question Answer 2:_____
NOTES:

Site URL:_____

Username:_____

Password:_____

Security Question Answer 1:_____

Security Question Answer 2:_____
NOTES:

Site URL:_____

Username:_____

Password:_____

Security Question Answer 1:_____

Security Question Answer 2:_____
NOTES:

Site URL:_____

Username:_____

Password:_____

Security Question Answer 1:_____

Security Question Answer 2:_____
NOTES:

Site URL:_____

Username:_____

Password:_____

Security Question Answer 1:_____

Security Question Answer 2:_____
NOTES:

Site URL:_____

Username:_____

Password:_____

Security Question Answer 1:_____

Security Question Answer 2:_____
NOTES:

Site URL:_____

Username:_____

Password:_____

Security Question Answer 1:_____

Security Question Answer 2:_____
NOTES:

Site URL:_____

Username:_____

Password:_____

Security Question Answer 1:_____

Security Question Answer 2:_____
NOTES:

Site URL:_____

Username:_____

Password:_____

Security Question Answer 1:_____

Security Question Answer 2:_____
NOTES:

Site URL:_____

Username:_____

Password:_____

Security Question Answer 1:_____

Security Question Answer 2:_____
NOTES:

Site URL:_____

Username:_____

Password:_____

Security Question Answer 1:_____

Security Question Answer 2:_____
NOTES:

Site URL:_____

Username:_____

Password:_____

Security Question Answer 1:_____

Security Question Answer 2:_____
NOTES:

Site URL:_____

Username:_____

Password:_____

Security Question Answer 1:_____

Security Question Answer 2:_____
NOTES:

Site URL:_____

Username:_____

Password:_____

Security Question Answer 1:_____

Security Question Answer 2:_____
NOTES:

Site URL:_____

Username:_____

Password:_____

Security Question Answer 1:_____

Security Question Answer 2:_____
NOTES:

Site URL:_____

Username:_____

Password:_____

Security Question Answer 1:_____

Security Question Answer 2:_____
NOTES:

Site URL:_____

Username:_____

Password:_____

Security Question Answer 1:_____

Security Question Answer 2:_____
NOTES:

Site URL:_____

Username:_____

Password:_____

Security Question Answer 1:_____

Security Question Answer 2:_____
NOTES:

Site URL:_____

Username:_____

Password:_____

Security Question Answer 1:_____

Security Question Answer 2:_____
NOTES:

Site URL:_____

Username:_____

Password:_____

Security Question Answer 1:_____

Security Question Answer 2:_____
NOTES:

Site URL:_____

Username:_____

Password:_____

Security Question Answer 1:_____

Security Question Answer 2:_____
NOTES:

Site URL:_____

Username:_____

Password:_____

Security Question Answer 1:_____

Security Question Answer 2:_____
NOTES:

Site URL:_____

Username:_____

Password:_____

Security Question Answer 1:_____

Security Question Answer 2:_____
NOTES:

Site URL:_____

Username:_____

Password:_____

Security Question Answer 1:_____

Security Question Answer 2:_____
NOTES:

Site URL:_____

Username:_____

Password:_____

Security Question Answer 1:_____

Security Question Answer 2:_____
NOTES:

Site URL:_____

Username:_____

Password:_____

Security Question Answer 1:_____

Security Question Answer 2:_____
NOTES:

Site URL:_____

Username:_____

Password:_____

Security Question Answer 1:_____

Security Question Answer 2:_____
NOTES:

Site URL:_____

Username:_____

Password:_____

Security Question Answer 1:_____

Security Question Answer 2:_____
NOTES:

Site URL:_____

Username:_____

Password:_____

Security Question Answer 1:_____

Security Question Answer 2:_____
NOTES:

Site URL:_____

Username:_____

Password:_____

Security Question Answer 1:_____

Security Question Answer 2:_____
NOTES:

Site URL:_____

Username:_____

Password:_____

Security Question Answer 1:_____

Security Question Answer 2:_____
NOTES:

Site URL:_____

Username:_____

Password:_____

Security Question Answer 1:_____

Security Question Answer 2:_____
NOTES:

Site URL:_____

Username:_____

Password:_____

Security Question Answer 1:_____

Security Question Answer 2:_____
NOTES:

Site URL:_____

Username:_____

Password:_____

Security Question Answer 1:_____

Security Question Answer 2:_____
NOTES:

Site URL:_____

Username:_____

Password:_____

Security Question Answer 1:_____

Security Question Answer 2:_____
NOTES:

Site URL:_____

Username:_____

Password:_____

Security Question Answer 1:_____

Security Question Answer 2:_____
NOTES:

Site URL:_____

Username:_____

Password:_____

Security Question Answer 1:_____

Security Question Answer 2:_____
NOTES:

Site URL:_____

Username:_____

Password:_____

Security Question Answer 1:_____

Security Question Answer 2:_____
NOTES:

Site URL:_____

Username:_____

Password:_____

Security Question Answer 1:_____

Security Question Answer 2:_____
NOTES:

Site URL:_____ _____

Username:_____ _____

Password:_____ _____

Security Question Answer 1:_____

Security Question Answer 2:_____
NOTES:

Site URL:_____

Username:_____

Password:_____

Security Question Answer 1:_____

Security Question Answer 2:_____
NOTES:

Site URL:_____

Username:_____

Password:_____

Security Question Answer 1:_____

Security Question Answer 2:_____
NOTES:

Site URL:_____

Username:_____

Password:_____

Security Question Answer 1:_____

Security Question Answer 2:_____
NOTES:

Site URL:_____

Username:_____

Password:_____

Security Question Answer 1:_____

Security Question Answer 2:_____
NOTES:

Site URL:_____

Username:_____

Password:_____

Security Question Answer 1:_____

Security Question Answer 2:_____
NOTES:

Site URL:_____

Username:_____

Password:_____

Security Question Answer 1:_____

Security Question Answer 2:_____
NOTES:

Site URL:_____

Username:_____

Password:_____

Security Question Answer 1:_____

Security Question Answer 2:_____
NOTES:

Site URL:_____

Username:_____

Password:_____

Security Question Answer 1:_____

Security Question Answer 2:_____
NOTES:

Site URL:_____

Username:_____

Password:_____

Security Question Answer 1:_____

Security Question Answer 2:_____
NOTES:

Site URL:_____

Username:_____

Password:_____

Security Question Answer 1:_____

Security Question Answer 2:_____
NOTES:

Site URL:_____

Username:_____

Password:_____

Security Question Answer 1:_____

Security Question Answer 2:_____
NOTES:

Site URL:_____

Username:_____

Password:_____

Security Question Answer 1:_____

Security Question Answer 2:_____
NOTES:

Site URL:_____

Username:_____

Password:_____

Security Question Answer 1:_____

Security Question Answer 2:_____
NOTES:

Site URL:_____

Username:_____

Password:_____

Security Question Answer 1:_____

Security Question Answer 2:_____
NOTES:

Site URL:_____

Username:_____

Password:_____

Security Question Answer 1:_____

Security Question Answer 2:_____
NOTES:

Site URL:_____

Username:_____

Password:_____

Security Question Answer 1:_____

Security Question Answer 2:_____
NOTES:

Site URL:_____

Username:_____

Password:_____

Security Question Answer 1:_____

Security Question Answer 2:_____
NOTES:

Site URL:_____

Username:_____

Password:_____

Security Question Answer 1:_____

Security Question Answer 2:_____
NOTES:

Site URL:_____

Username:_____

Password:_____

Security Question Answer 1:_____

Security Question Answer 2:_____
NOTES:

Site URL:_____

Username:_____

Password:_____

Security Question Answer 1:_____

Security Question Answer 2:_____
NOTES:

Site URL:_____

Username:_____

Password:_____

Security Question Answer 1:_____

Security Question Answer 2:_____
NOTES:

Site URL:_____

Username:_____

Password:_____

Security Question Answer 1:_____

Security Question Answer 2:_____
NOTES:

Site URL:_____

Username:_____

Password:_____

Security Question Answer 1:_____

Security Question Answer 2:_____
NOTES:

Site URL:_____

Username:_____

Password:_____

Security Question Answer 1:_____

Security Question Answer 2:_____
NOTES:

Site URL:_____

Username:_____

Password:_____

Security Question Answer 1:_____

Security Question Answer 2:_____
NOTES:

Site URL:_____

Username:_____

Password:_____

Security Question Answer 1:_____

Security Question Answer 2:_____
NOTES:

Site URL:_____

Username:_____

Password:_____

Security Question Answer 1:_____

Security Question Answer 2:_____
NOTES:

Site URL:_____

Username:_____

Password:_____

Security Question Answer 1:_____

Security Question Answer 2:_____
NOTES:

Site URL:_____

Username:_____

Password:_____

Security Question Answer 1:_____

Security Question Answer 2:_____
NOTES:

Site URL:_____

Username:_____

Password:_____

Security Question Answer 1:_____

Security Question Answer 2:_____
NOTES:

Site URL:_____

Username:_____

Password:_____

Security Question Answer 1:_____

Security Question Answer 2:_____
NOTES:

Site URL:_____

Username:_____

Password:_____

Security Question Answer 1:_____

Security Question Answer 2:_____
NOTES:

Site URL:_____

Username:_____

Password:_____

Security Question Answer 1:_____

Security Question Answer 2:_____
NOTES:

Site URL:_____

Username:_____

Password:_____

Security Question Answer 1:_____

Security Question Answer 2:_____
NOTES:

Site URL:_____

Username:_____

Password:_____

Security Question Answer 1:_____

Security Question Answer 2:_____
NOTES:

Site URL:_____

Username:_____

Password:_____

Security Question Answer 1:_____

Security Question Answer 2:_____
NOTES:

Site URL:_____

Username:_____

Password:_____

Security Question Answer 1:_____

Security Question Answer 2:_____
NOTES:

Site URL:_____

Username:_____

Password:_____

Security Question Answer 1:_____

Security Question Answer 2:_____
NOTES:

Site URL:_____

Username:_____

Password:_____

Security Question Answer 1:_____

Security Question Answer 2:_____
NOTES:

Site URL:_____

Username:_____

Password:_____

Security Question Answer 1:_____

Security Question Answer 2:_____
NOTES:

Site URL:_____

Username:_____

Password:_____

Security Question Answer 1:_____

Security Question Answer 2:_____
NOTES:

Site URL:_____

Username:_____

Password:_____

Security Question Answer 1:_____

Security Question Answer 2:_____
NOTES:

Site URL:_____

Username:_____

Password:_____

Security Question Answer 1:_____

Security Question Answer 2:_____
NOTES:

Site URL:_____

Username:_____

Password:_____

Security Question Answer 1:_____

Security Question Answer 2:_____
NOTES:

Site URL:_____

Username:_____

Password:_____

Security Question Answer 1:_____

Security Question Answer 2:_____
NOTES:

Site URL:_____

Username:_____

Password:_____

Security Question Answer 1:_____

Security Question Answer 2:_____
NOTES:

Site URL:_____

Username:_____

Password:_____

Security Question Answer 1:_____

Security Question Answer 2:_____
NOTES:

Site URL:_____

Username:_____

Password:_____

Security Question Answer 1:_____

Security Question Answer 2:_____
NOTES:

Site URL:_____

Username:_____

Password:_____

Security Question Answer 1:_____

Security Question Answer 2:_____
NOTES:

Site URL:_____

Username:_____

Password:_____

Security Question Answer 1:_____

Security Question Answer 2:_____
NOTES:

Site URL:_____

Username:_____

Password:_____

Security Question Answer 1:_____

Security Question Answer 2:_____
NOTES:

Site URL:_____

Username:_____

Password:_____

Security Question Answer 1:_____

Security Question Answer 2:_____
NOTES:

Site URL:_____

Username:_____

Password:_____

Security Question Answer 1:_____

Security Question Answer 2:_____
NOTES:

Site URL:_____

Username:_____

Password:_____

Security Question Answer 1:_____

Security Question Answer 2:_____
NOTES:

Site URL:_____

Username:_____

Password:_____

Security Question Answer 1:_____

Security Question Answer 2:_____
NOTES:

Site URL:_____

Username:_____

Password:_____

Security Question Answer 1:_____

Security Question Answer 2:_____
NOTES:

Site URL:_____

Username:_____

Password:_____

Security Question Answer 1:_____

Security Question Answer 2:_____
NOTES:

Site URL:_____

Username:_____

Password:_____

Security Question Answer 1:_____

Security Question Answer 2:_____
NOTES:

Site URL:_____

Username:_____

Password:_____

Security Question Answer 1:_____

Security Question Answer 2:_____
NOTES:

Site URL:_____

Username:_____

Password:_____

Security Question Answer 1:_____

Security Question Answer 2:_____
NOTES:

Site URL:_____

Username:_____

Password:_____

Security Question Answer 1:_____

Security Question Answer 2:_____
NOTES:

Site URL:_____

Username:_____

Password:_____

Security Question Answer 1:_____

Security Question Answer 2:_____
NOTES:

Site URL:_____ _____

Username:_____ _____

Password:_____

Security Question Answer 1:_____

Security Question Answer 2:_____
NOTES:

Site URL:_____

Username:_____

Password:_____

Security Question Answer 1:_____

Security Question Answer 2:_____
NOTES:

Site URL:_____

Username:_____

Password:_____

Security Question Answer 1:_____

Security Question Answer 2:_____
NOTES:

Site URL:_____

Username:_____

Password:_____

Security Question Answer 1:_____

Security Question Answer 2:_____
NOTES:

Site URL:_____

Username:_____

Password:_____

Security Question Answer 1:_____

Security Question Answer 2:_____
NOTES:

Site URL:_____

Username:_____

Password:_____

Security Question Answer 1:_____

Security Question Answer 2:_____
NOTES:

Site URL:_____

Username:_____

Password:_____

Security Question Answer 1:_____

Security Question Answer 2:_____
NOTES:

Site URL:_____

Username:_____

Password:_____

Security Question Answer 1:_____

Security Question Answer 2:_____
NOTES:

Site URL:_____

Username:_____

Password:_____

Security Question Answer 1:_____

Security Question Answer 2:_____
NOTES:

Site URL:_____

Username:_____

Password:_____

Security Question Answer 1:_____

Security Question Answer 2:_____
NOTES:

Site URL:_____

Username:_____

Password:_____

Security Question Answer 1:_____

Security Question Answer 2:_____
NOTES:

Site URL:_____

Username:_____

Password:_____

Security Question Answer 1:_____

Security Question Answer 2:_____
NOTES:

Site URL:_____

Username:_____

Password:_____

Security Question Answer 1:_____

Security Question Answer 2:_____
NOTES:

Site URL:_____

Username:_____

Password:_____

Security Question Answer 1:_____

Security Question Answer 2:_____
NOTES:

Site URL:_____

Username:_____

Password:_____

Security Question Answer 1:_____

Security Question Answer 2:_____
NOTES:

Site URL:_____

Username:_____

Password:_____

Security Question Answer 1:_____

Security Question Answer 2:_____
NOTES:

Site URL:_____

Username:_____

Password:_____

Security Question Answer 1:_____

Security Question Answer 2:_____
NOTES:

Site URL:_____

Username:_____

Password:_____

Security Question Answer 1:_____

Security Question Answer 2:_____
NOTES:

Site URL:_____

Username:_____

Password:_____

Security Question Answer 1:_____

Security Question Answer 2:_____
NOTES:

Site URL:_____

Username:_____

Password:_____

Security Question Answer 1:_____

Security Question Answer 2:_____
NOTES:

Site URL:_____

Username:_____

Password:_____

Security Question Answer 1:_____

Security Question Answer 2:_____
NOTES:

Site URL:_____

Username:_____

Password:_____

Security Question Answer 1:_____

Security Question Answer 2:_____
NOTES:

Site URL:_____

Username:_____

Password:_____

Security Question Answer 1:_____

Security Question Answer 2:_____
NOTES:

Site URL:_____

Username:_____

Password:_____

Security Question Answer 1:_____

Security Question Answer 2:_____
NOTES:

Site URL:_____

Username:_____

Password:_____

Security Question Answer 1:_____

Security Question Answer 2:_____
NOTES:

Site URL:_____

Username:_____

Password:_____

Security Question Answer 1:_____

Security Question Answer 2:_____
NOTES:

Site URL:_____

Username:_____

Password:_____

Security Question Answer 1:_____

Security Question Answer 2:_____
NOTES:

Site URL:_____

Username:_____

Password:_____

Security Question Answer 1:_____

Security Question Answer 2:_____
NOTES:

Site URL:_____

Username:_____

Password:_____

Security Question Answer 1:_____

Security Question Answer 2:_____
NOTES:

Site URL:_____

Username:_____

Password:_____

Security Question Answer 1:_____

Security Question Answer 2:_____
NOTES:

Site URL:_____

Username:_____

Password:_____

Security Question Answer 1:_____

Security Question Answer 2:_____
NOTES:

Site URL:_____

Username:_____

Password:_____

Security Question Answer 1:_____

Security Question Answer 2:_____
NOTES:

Site URL:_____

Username:_____

Password:_____

Security Question Answer 1:_____

Security Question Answer 2:_____
NOTES:

Site URL:_____

Username:_____

Password:_____

Security Question Answer 1:_____

Security Question Answer 2:_____
NOTES:

Site URL:_____

Username:_____

Password:_____

Security Question Answer 1:_____

Security Question Answer 2:_____
NOTES:

Site URL:_____

Username:_____

Password:_____

Security Question Answer 1:_____

Security Question Answer 2:_____
NOTES:

Site URL:_____

Username:_____

Password:_____

Security Question Answer 1:_____

Security Question Answer 2:_____
NOTES:

Site URL:_____

Username:_____

Password:_____

Security Question Answer 1:_____

Security Question Answer 2:_____
NOTES:

Site URL:_____

Username:_____

Password:_____

Security Question Answer 1:_____

Security Question Answer 2:_____
NOTES:

Site URL:_____

Username:_____

Password:_____

Security Question Answer 1:_____

Security Question Answer 2:_____
NOTES:

Site URL:_____

Username:_____

Password:_____

Security Question Answer 1:_____

Security Question Answer 2:_____
NOTES:

Site URL:_____

Username:_____

Password:_____

Security Question Answer 1:_____

Security Question Answer 2:_____
NOTES:

Site URL:_____

Username:_____

Password:_____

Security Question Answer 1:_____

Security Question Answer 2:_____
NOTES:

Site URL:_____

Username:_____

Password:_____

Security Question Answer 1:_____

Security Question Answer 2:_____
NOTES:

Site URL:_____

Username:_____

Password:_____

Security Question Answer 1:_____

Security Question Answer 2:_____
NOTES:

Site URL:_____

Username:_____

Password:_____

Security Question Answer 1:_____

Security Question Answer 2:_____
NOTES:

Site URL:_____

Username:_____

Password:_____

Security Question Answer 1:_____

Security Question Answer 2:_____
NOTES:

Site URL:_____

Username:_____

Password:_____

Security Question Answer 1:_____

Security Question Answer 2:_____
NOTES:

Site URL:_____

Username:_____

Password:_____

Security Question Answer 1:_____

Security Question Answer 2:_____
NOTES:

Site URL:_____

Username:_____

Password:_____

Security Question Answer 1:_____

Security Question Answer 2:_____
NOTES:

Site URL:_____

Username:_____

Password:_____

Security Question Answer 1:_____

Security Question Answer 2:_____
NOTES:

Site URL:_____

Username:_____

Password:_____

Security Question Answer 1:_____

Security Question Answer 2:_____
NOTES:

Site URL:_____

Username:_____

Password:_____

Security Question Answer 1:_____

Security Question Answer 2:_____
NOTES:

Site URL:_____

Username:_____

Password:_____

Security Question Answer 1:_____

Security Question Answer 2:_____
NOTES:

Site URL:_____

Username:_____

Password:_____

Security Question Answer 1:_____

Security Question Answer 2:_____
NOTES:

Site URL:_____

Username:_____

Password:_____

Security Question Answer 1:_____

Security Question Answer 2:_____
NOTES:

Site URL:_____

Username:_____

Password:_____

Security Question Answer 1:_____

Security Question Answer 2:_____
NOTES:

Site URL:_____

Username:_____

Password:_____

Security Question Answer 1:_____

Security Question Answer 2:_____
NOTES:

Site URL:_____

Username:_____

Password:_____

Security Question Answer 1:_____

Security Question Answer 2:_____
NOTES:

Site URL:_____

Username:_____

Password:_____

Security Question Answer 1:_____

Security Question Answer 2:_____
NOTES:

Site URL:_____

Username:_____

Password:_____

Security Question Answer 1:_____

Security Question Answer 2:_____
NOTES:

Site URL:_____

Username:_____

Password:_____

Security Question Answer 1:_____

Security Question Answer 2:_____
NOTES:

Site URL:_____

Username:_____

Password:_____

Security Question Answer 1:_____

Security Question Answer 2:_____
NOTES:

Site URL:_____

Username:_____

Password:_____

Security Question Answer 1:_____

Security Question Answer 2:_____
NOTES:

Site URL:_____

Username:_____

Password:_____

Security Question Answer 1:_____

Security Question Answer 2:_____
NOTES:

Site URL:_____

Username:_____

Password:_____

Security Question Answer 1:_____

Security Question Answer 2:_____
NOTES:

Site URL:_____

Username:_____

Password:_____

Security Question Answer 1:_____

Security Question Answer 2:_____
NOTES:

Site URL:_____

Username:_____

Password:_____

Security Question Answer 1:_____

Security Question Answer 2:_____
NOTES:

Site URL:_____

Username:_____

Password:_____

Security Question Answer 1:_____

Security Question Answer 2:_____
NOTES:

Site URL:_____

Username:_____

Password:_____

Security Question Answer 1:_____

Security Question Answer 2:_____
NOTES:

Site URL:_____

Username:_____

Password:_____

Security Question Answer 1:_____

Security Question Answer 2:_____
NOTES:

Site URL:_____

Username:_____

Password:_____

Security Question Answer 1:_____

Security Question Answer 2:_____
NOTES:

Site URL:_____

Username:_____

Password:_____

Security Question Answer 1:_____

Security Question Answer 2:_____
NOTES:

Site URL:_____

Username:_____

Password:_____

Security Question Answer 1:_____

Security Question Answer 2:_____
NOTES:

Site URL:_____

Username:_____

Password:_____

Security Question Answer 1:_____

Security Question Answer 2:_____
NOTES:

Site URL:_____

Username:_____

Password:_____

Security Question Answer 1:_____

Security Question Answer 2:_____
NOTES:

Site URL:_____

Username:_____

Password:_____

Security Question Answer 1:_____

Security Question Answer 2:_____
NOTES:

Site URL:_____

Username:_____

Password:_____

Security Question Answer 1:_____

Security Question Answer 2:_____
NOTES:

Site URL:_____

Username:_____

Password:_____

Security Question Answer 1:_____

Security Question Answer 2:_____
NOTES:

Site URL:_____

Username:_____

Password:_____

Security Question Answer 1:_____

Security Question Answer 2:_____
NOTES:

Site URL:_____

Username:_____

Password:_____

Security Question Answer 1:_____

Security Question Answer 2:_____
NOTES:

Site URL:_____

Username:_____

Password:_____

Security Question Answer 1:_____

Security Question Answer 2:_____
NOTES:

Site URL:_____

Username:_____

Password:_____

Security Question Answer 1:_____

Security Question Answer 2:_____
NOTES:

Site URL:_____

Username:_____

Password:_____

Security Question Answer 1:_____

Security Question Answer 2:_____
NOTES:

Site URL:_____

Username:_____

Password:_____

Security Question Answer 1:_____

Security Question Answer 2:_____
NOTES:

Site URL:_____

Username:_____

Password:_____

Security Question Answer 1:_____

Security Question Answer 2:_____
NOTES:

Site URL:_____

Username:_____

Password:_____

Security Question Answer 1:_____

Security Question Answer 2:_____
NOTES:

Site URL:_____

Username:_____

Password:_____

Security Question Answer 1:_____

Security Question Answer 2:_____
NOTES:

Site URL:_____

Username:_____

Password:_____

Security Question Answer 1:_____

Security Question Answer 2:_____
NOTES:

Site URL:_____

Username:_____

Password:_____

Security Question Answer 1:_____

Security Question Answer 2:_____
NOTES:

Site URL:_____

Username:_____

Password:_____

Security Question Answer 1:_____

Security Question Answer 2:_____
NOTES:

Site URL:_____

Username:_____

Password:_____

Security Question Answer 1:_____

Security Question Answer 2:_____
NOTES:

Site URL:_____

Username:_____

Password:_____

Security Question Answer 1:_____

Security Question Answer 2:_____
NOTES:

Site URL:_____

Username:_____

Password:_____

Security Question Answer 1:_____

Security Question Answer 2:_____
NOTES:

Site URL:_____

Username:_____

Password:_____

Security Question Answer 1:_____

Security Question Answer 2:_____
NOTES:

Site URL:_____

Username:_____

Password:_____

Security Question Answer 1:_____

Security Question Answer 2:_____
NOTES:

Site URL:_____

Username:_____

Password:_____

Security Question Answer 1:_____

Security Question Answer 2:_____
NOTES:

Site URL:_____

Username:_____

Password:_____

Security Question Answer 1:_____

Security Question Answer 2:_____
NOTES:

Site URL:_____

Username:_____

Password:_____

Security Question Answer 1:_____

Security Question Answer 2:_____
NOTES:

Site URL:_____

Username:_____

Password:_____

Security Question Answer 1:_____

Security Question Answer 2:_____
NOTES:

Site URL:_____

Username:_____

Password:_____

Security Question Answer 1:_____

Security Question Answer 2:_____
NOTES:

Site URL:_____

Username:_____

Password:_____

Security Question Answer 1:_____

Security Question Answer 2:_____
NOTES:

Site URL:_____

Username:_____

Password:_____

Security Question Answer 1:_____

Security Question Answer 2:_____
NOTES:

Site URL:_____

Username:_____

Password:_____

Security Question Answer 1:_____

Security Question Answer 2:_____
NOTES:

Site URL:_____

Username:_____

Password:_____

Security Question Answer 1:_____

Security Question Answer 2:_____
NOTES:

Site URL:_____

Username:_____

Password:_____

Security Question Answer 1:_____

Security Question Answer 2:_____
NOTES:

Site URL:_____

Username:_____

Password:_____

Security Question Answer 1:_____

Security Question Answer 2:_____
NOTES:

Site URL:_____

Username:_____

Password:_____

Security Question Answer 1:_____

Security Question Answer 2:_____
NOTES:

Site URL:_____

Username:_____

Password:_____

Security Question Answer 1:_____

Security Question Answer 2:_____
NOTES:

Site URL:_____

Username:_____

Password:_____

Security Question Answer 1:_____

Security Question Answer 2:_____
NOTES:

Site URL:_____

Username:_____

Password:_____

Security Question Answer 1:_____

Security Question Answer 2:_____
NOTES:

Site URL:_____

Username:_____

Password:_____

Security Question Answer 1:_____

Security Question Answer 2:_____
NOTES:

Site URL:_____

Username:_____

Password:_____

Security Question Answer 1:_____

Security Question Answer 2:_____
NOTES:

Site URL:_____

Username:_____

Password:_____

Security Question Answer 1:_____

Security Question Answer 2:_____
NOTES:

Site URL:_____

Username:_____

Password:_____

Security Question Answer 1:_____

Security Question Answer 2:_____
NOTES:

Site URL:_____

Username:_____

Password:_____

Security Question Answer 1:_____

Security Question Answer 2:_____
NOTES:

Site URL:_____

Username:_____

Password:_____

Security Question Answer 1:_____

Security Question Answer 2:_____
NOTES:

Site URL:_____

Username:_____

Password:_____

Security Question Answer 1:_____

Security Question Answer 2:_____
NOTES:

Site URL:_____

Username:_____

Password:_____

Security Question Answer 1:_____

Security Question Answer 2:_____
NOTES:

Site URL:_____

Username:_____

Password:_____

Security Question Answer 1:_____

Security Question Answer 2:_____
NOTES:

Site URL:_____

Username:_____

Password:_____

Security Question Answer 1:_____

Security Question Answer 2:_____
NOTES:

Site URL:_____

Username:_____

Password:_____

Security Question Answer 1:_____

Security Question Answer 2:_____
NOTES:

Site URL:_____

Username:_____

Password:_____

Security Question Answer 1:_____

Security Question Answer 2:_____
NOTES:

Site URL:_____

Username:_____

Password:_____

Security Question Answer 1:_____

Security Question Answer 2:_____
NOTES:

Site URL:_____

Username:_____

Password:_____

Security Question Answer 1:_____

Security Question Answer 2:_____
NOTES:

Site URL:_____

Username:_____

Password:_____

Security Question Answer 1:_____

Security Question Answer 2:_____
NOTES:

Site URL:_____

Username:_____

Password:_____

Security Question Answer 1:_____

Security Question Answer 2:_____
NOTES:

Site URL:_____

Username:_____

Password:_____

Security Question Answer 1:_____

Security Question Answer 2:_____
NOTES:

Site URL:_____

Username:_____

Password:_____

Security Question Answer 1:_____

Security Question Answer 2:_____
NOTES:

Site URL:_____

Username:_____

Password:_____

Security Question Answer 1:_____

Security Question Answer 2:_____
NOTES:

Site URL:_____

Username:_____

Password:_____

Security Question Answer 1:_____

Security Question Answer 2:_____
NOTES:

Site URL:_____

Username:_____

Password:_____

Security Question Answer 1:_____

Security Question Answer 2:_____
NOTES:

Site URL:_____

Username:_____

Password:_____

Security Question Answer 1:_____

Security Question Answer 2:_____
NOTES:

Site URL:_____

Username:_____

Password:_____

Security Question Answer 1:_____

Security Question Answer 2:_____
NOTES:

Site URL:_____

Username:_____

Password:_____

Security Question Answer 1:_____

Security Question Answer 2:_____
NOTES:

Site URL:_____

Username:_____

Password:_____

Security Question Answer 1:_____

Security Question Answer 2:_____
NOTES:

Site URL:_____

Username:_____

Password:_____

Security Question Answer 1:_____

Security Question Answer 2:_____
NOTES:

Site URL:_____

Username:_____

Password:_____

Security Question Answer 1:_____

Security Question Answer 2:_____
NOTES:

Site URL:_____

Username:_____

Password:_____

Security Question Answer 1:_____

Security Question Answer 2:_____
NOTES:

Site URL:_____

Username:_____

Password:_____

Security Question Answer 1:_____

Security Question Answer 2:_____
NOTES:

Site URL:_____

Username:_____

Password:_____

Security Question Answer 1:_____

Security Question Answer 2:_____
NOTES:

Site URL:_____

Username:_____

Password:_____

Security Question Answer 1:_____

Security Question Answer 2:_____
NOTES:

Site URL:_____

Username:_____

Password:_____

Security Question Answer 1:_____

Security Question Answer 2:_____
NOTES:

Site URL:_____

Username:_____

Password:_____

Security Question Answer 1:_____

Security Question Answer 2:_____
NOTES:

Site URL:_____

Username:_____

Password:_____

Security Question Answer 1:_____

Security Question Answer 2:_____
NOTES:

Site URL:_____

Username:_____

Password:_____

Security Question Answer 1:_____

Security Question Answer 2:_____
NOTES:

Site URL:_____

Username:_____

Password:_____

Security Question Answer 1:_____

Security Question Answer 2:_____
NOTES:

Site URL:_____ _____

Username:_____ ___

Password:_____ __

Security Question Answer 1:_____

Security Question Answer 2:_____
NOTES:

Site URL:_____ ___

Username:_____ ___

Password:_____ _

Security Question Answer 1:_____

Security Question Answer 2:_____
NOTES:

Site URL:_____ ___

Username:_____ ___

Password:_____ __

Security Question Answer 1:_____

Security Question Answer 2:_____
NOTES:

Site URL:_____

Username:_____

Password:_____

Security Question Answer 1:_____

Security Question Answer 2:_____
NOTES:

Site URL:_____

Username:_____

Password:_____

Security Question Answer 1:_____

Security Question Answer 2:_____
NOTES:

Site URL:_____

Username:_____

Password:_____

Security Question Answer 1:_____

Security Question Answer 2:_____
NOTES:

Site URL:_____

Username:_____

Password:_____

Security Question Answer 1:_____

Security Question Answer 2:_____
NOTES:

Site URL:_____

Username:_____

Password:_____

Security Question Answer 1:_____

Security Question Answer 2:_____
NOTES:

Site URL:_____

Username:_____

Password:_____

Security Question Answer 1:_____

Security Question Answer 2:_____
NOTES:

Site URL:_____

Username:_____

Password:_____

Security Question Answer 1:_____

Security Question Answer 2:_____
NOTES:

Site URL:_____

Username:_____

Password:_____

Security Question Answer 1:_____

Security Question Answer 2:_____
NOTES:

Site URL:_____

Username:_____

Password:_____

Security Question Answer 1:_____

Security Question Answer 2:_____
NOTES:

Site URL:_____

Username:_____

Password:_____

Security Question Answer 1:_____

Security Question Answer 2:_____
NOTES:

Site URL:_____

Username:_____

Password:_____

Security Question Answer 1:_____

Security Question Answer 2:_____
NOTES:

Site URL:_____

Username:_____

Password:_____

Security Question Answer 1:_____

Security Question Answer 2:_____
NOTES:

Site URL:_____

Username:_____

Password:_____

Security Question Answer 1:_____

Security Question Answer 2:_____
NOTES:

Site URL:_____

Username:_____

Password:_____

Security Question Answer 1:_____

Security Question Answer 2:_____
NOTES:

Site URL:_____

Username:_____

Password:_____

Security Question Answer 1:_____

Security Question Answer 2:_____
NOTES:

Site URL:_____

Username:_____

Password:_____

Security Question Answer 1:_____

Security Question Answer 2:_____
NOTES:

Site URL:_____

Username:_____

Password:_____

Security Question Answer 1:_____

Security Question Answer 2:_____
NOTES:

Site URL:_____

Username:_____

Password:_____

Security Question Answer 1:_____

Security Question Answer 2:_____
NOTES:

Site URL:_____

Username:_____

Password:_____

Security Question Answer 1:_____

Security Question Answer 2:_____
NOTES:

Site URL:_____

Username:_____

Password:_____

Security Question Answer 1:_____

Security Question Answer 2:_____
NOTES:

Site URL:_____

Username:_____

Password:_____

Security Question Answer 1:_____

Security Question Answer 2:_____
NOTES:

Site URL:_____

Username:_____

Password:_____

Security Question Answer 1:_____

Security Question Answer 2:_____
NOTES:

Site URL:_____

Username:_____

Password:_____

Security Question Answer 1:_____

Security Question Answer 2:_____
NOTES:

Site URL:_____

Username:_____

Password:_____

Security Question Answer 1:_____

Security Question Answer 2:_____
NOTES:

Other Accounts

`*******`

Internet Service Provider: _____

My Account Number:_____

Tech Support Number:_____

Customer Service Number:_____

Email:_____

My Main Email Account:_____

Password:_____

Security Question Answer 1:_____

Security Question Answer 2:_____

Notes:

My Alternate Email Account:_____

Password:_____

Security Question Answer 1:_____

Security Question Answer 2:_____

Notes:

Bank Account Company:_____

Type of Account:_____

Account Number:_____

PIN:_____

Routing Number (Checking):_____

Bank Account Company:_____

Type of Account:_____

Account Number:_____

PIN:_____

Routing Number (Checking):_____

Other Accounts

****

Bank Account Company:_____

Type of Account:_____

Account Number:_____

PIN:_____

Routing Number (Checking):_____

Credit Card: _____

My Account Number:_____

PIN:_____

Customer Service Number:_____

Email:_____

Credit Card: _____

My Account Number:_____

PIN:_____

Customer Service Number:_____

Email:_____

Credit Card: _____

My Account Number:_____

PIN:_____

Customer Service Number:_____

Email:_____

Credit Card: _____

My Account Number:_____

PIN:_____

Customer Service Number:_____

Email:_____

Handy Tips

When it comes to safeguarding your personal information, use due diligence, by making identity protection a daily habit.

Use substantial passwords for your online accounts. Your password doesn't have to be a word. It can be the first letter of each word in a phrase. For instance, the phrase 'these pretzels are making me thirsty' could translate to 'Tpammt.' It's a smart idea to also include a number or punctuation mark, such as an ! or a ; as part of your password.

If you have a log-in account created on a website that requires you to change your password periodically, you could add multiples of 5. So, your password might look something like Tpammt!5 or Tpammt!10.

Use a combination of upper and lowercase letters, if the site allows for it. This also creates an extra level of security when protecting your online account information. The goal is to use what works best for you while making it harder for hackers to hack your account.

Social Media

Be aware of what you share on social media. Identity thieves are known to patrol social media platforms to target unsuspecting people. If you are one of the millions of people that use social media to communicate with family and friends, it's a smart idea to periodically check the security features on the websites and only share your posts with people you know, such as friends and family. Don't post your full name (maiden name), phone number or address on websites that are publicly accessible.

Handy Tips

Email

When you create an account on a website, one of the first things you'll be asked for is your email address. Before you hand it over, consider using an email address that you designate specifically for other companies.

Using a separate email address for only friends and family helps cut down on the time spent weeding through *spam*, aka *email junk mail*.

Already have everything coming to one email address? Not to worry, you can still create a new email account from websites like Yahoo!, Gmail or similar free services. Give the new email address to friends and family so that you don't have to check the old email address unless you are expecting to have communication from one of the companies.

When it comes to internet safety, another way hackers can obtain access to your personal information is through a process called *spoofing*. Spoofing, also known as *phishing* is essentially an email that looks very similar to something a reputable company might send out. The email could go as far as even including a logo that looks much like a well known company's logo, in an attempt to better fool the receiver of the email. The email will most often include a link to a website that is infected with *malware* or a computer virus that allows the hacker to access usernames and passwords stored on your computer. Because of this, it is extremely important to be aware of recognizing legitimate versus fake email that comes into your inbox.

Never click on links, open files or download software programs sent to you from strangers.

Handy Tips

Even if the email appearance looks real, one of the surefire ways to know that an email is not legitimate is if you receive one asking for personal information. Reputable companies will not solicit you for this information. In fact, if you didn't initiate the contact, that is red flag warning number one. If a company sends you an email and asks for personal information, such as your social security number here in the United States, do not click on any link in the email. Instead, call the company directly using their customer service contact information and ask them if they sent the email.

Other types of phishing include:
Clone Phishing - a hacker gains access to a previously delivered email that has links or attachments and then creates a nearly identical email that can take control of your computer and then infect other computers through email that you send.

Spear Phishing - are attacks directed at a specific person or company. Spear fishing accounts for the majority of known attacks. Hackers obtain certain information about their target and use it as leverage in their attack.

Whaling - is a laser-focused electronic attack, aimed at upper level management within an organization. The emails have been known to include a fake subpoena and require the recipient to download what they are led to believe is special software to view the subpoena.

Website Safety
Of course, spoofing isn't limited to just emails. Hackers have also been known to construct websites that are made to look like trustworthy sites, too.

Handy Tips

If you shop online, it's best to shop from well-known and established websites, when giving your credit card information over the internet. When you shop using a credit card online in the United States, you are protected by the Fair Credit Billing Act. This law protects the consumer from fraudulent activity. allowing the consumer to dispute certain charges and temporarily withhold payment while the creditor initiates an investigation.

When placing an order or submitting payment information online, look in your browser's address bar. The website address should switch from http to https. The 's' stands for secure. Of course, nothing in this day and age is foolproof, so be sure to use common sense when submitting payment information through the internet.

A good rule of this is, if it looks suspicious, it probably is!

If you experience shopping fraud online, report it. File a formal complaint with the Federal Trade Commission *www.ftc.gov/complaint*, contact your state Attorney General office *naag.org* and the Better Business Bureau *www.bbb.org*. All three take internet fraud seriously and have special divisions assigned to help protect the consumer from falling victim to online financial predators.

WiFi Safety in Public Places
Free wireless internet access points are popping up all over the world. Whether you are downtown in a metropolitan area, at the local Starbucks or your community library, visitors can jump onto free internet access, known as WiFi.

Handy Tips

WiFi can be a less secure form of connecting to the internet, compared to wired connections, such as an Ethernet connection because a hacker doesn't need a physical connection to get into your computer. There are various encryption technologies in place to help combat fraudulent activity through WiFi.

Hotspots, a more commonplace term for wireless connection in a public place, are prime targets for hackers. Because of this, your data is at risk every time you connect to a hotspot.

Rogue WiFi is also another growing concern. Hackers set up their own hotspot in a public place, allow unsuspecting users to join on in order to access the internet. The hackers then run what is known as a man-in-the-middle (MitM) attack to the unsuspecting public WiFi users. The lesson here is, connect to a free WiFi hotspot only if you completely trust the source and even then, only do it if you must!

WiFi Safety at Home
If you access the internet at home wirelessly, consider taking the following precautions into consideration when setting up your WiFi:
Turn on the encryption - as of this writing, WPA2 is currently the strongest type of home encryption available. It is much more secure than using WEP.
Turn on the router firewall - Wireless routers often have the firewall turned off when they first come out of the packaging. Turn yours on for an extra level of internet security.
Change the password - Your wireless internet router comes with a preset password. Change the password (*and store it in this book!*) to a combination of letters, numbers and symbols for the best protection

Handy Tips

against having your home WiFi connection compromised. The longer the password combination, the harder it is to crack.

If you notice that your internet connection seems slower than normal, it's a sign that someone within range of your network has successfully logged onto it and is using your bandwidth for free; the very bandwidth that you have to pay for every month. If that happens, change your WiFi password (*and don't forget to update it in this book!*).

Create a Unique Network Name – How often have you seen your neighbor's WiFi on your local list of local networks to connect to? It's not uncommon for people to use their last name for their network name, but why make it easy for people in your area to know which network is yours? Remember, identity theft is rampant in this day and age. Don't name your network something that anyone within range will know that it's yours. Have fun with the name. It doesn't even have to make sense. Just name it something that isn't necessarily easily traced to your home. Don't use a family member's name or a pet's name. Come up with something unrelated to you or your interests.

Disable Network Identifier Broadcasting – Broadcasting your home network's name isn't even necessary in most instances, so turn that feature off on your router. If someone doesn't know you have a wireless router, then it's less likely you will be a target for network hacking.

Create a MAC Address Filter – Doing so is yet another level of security for your home network and allows you to approve devices that are allowed to connect wirelessly.

Handy Tips

What to Do if You are Hacked

If you notice that your Sent folder in your email program contains messages in it that you didn't send, that's a surefire sign that you have been hacked. Have friends and family received emails or online social media messages made to look like they came from you, but that you didn't send? That is one of the most common telltale signs that you have fallen victim to a hacker.

You should immediately update your computer security software and remove any malware that may have been installed. If you don't have computer security software installed, now would be a good time to purchase some from a reputable company such as Norton. Run a scan on your computer with the software and remove any suspicious software programs. Be sure to reboot your computer so that the changes are fully recognized.

Change your passwords. Yes, this can be a real hassle, but if your computer has been hacked, then it's a necessity. If you already have your passwords entered into this book, then you can just go through each page and update the sites you have accounts set up on.

If you've been locked out of your social media accounts because of a hacker, then it's best to consult the site's policy on restoring access to an account. You may be required to supply the company with identifiable information in order to prove that you are really the account holder and some sites might require you to submit a form in order for you to regain access to your account.

Knowledge is power and the more you know, the better prepared you will become if you are ever the target of internet hackers.

Notes

Notes

Notes

Printed in Great Britain
by Amazon.co.uk, Ltd.,
Marston Gate.